Peace

Fruit of the Spirit
PEACE

YOUR DAILY MEDITATION

SISTER IRINI

Bible references (*Italics*): New Revised Standard Version Updated Edition (NRSVUE) from bible gateway.com

Cover Design: Lovo.Ai Virtual Art
Editing: Chat GPT 4
ISBN:9781738622399

SEASEM PUBLICATIONS
publications@seasem.org

Peace I leave with you. My peace I give to you.

John 14:27

Contents

Introduction

Peace is the forerunner of all fruit of the Spirit. Peace is the steady foundation upon which the presence of the Spirit is realised; the tranquil soil from which love, joy, patience, kindness, and all other fruit take root in our lives. This peace is no ordinary peace; it is the peace of Jesus Christ Himself, the 'Prince of Peace' (Isaiah 9:6). In Christ, we encounter this peace that is not fleeting or dependent on external circumstances but is an abiding presence dwelling within us, creating a lasting sanctuary where the soul can commune in the presence and works of the Holy Spirit.

The peace that Jesus leaves us with is fundamentally different from worldly peace—rooted as it is in our reconciliation with

God, and our relationship with Jesus Christ. Our trust in God's sovereignty, and in Christ's life, death and resurrection secures victory for us over death, ensuring eternal life, liberating us from fear and anxiety, and all worldly concerns. The breath of this glorious peace dwells in us offering itself to us through the Holy Spirit, whom God sent to us to make Christ's presence active within us. It is Christ's peace that you will encounter in this month of divine reflection.

Fruit of the Spirit

We are all called to love, joy, peace, patience, kindness, generosity, faithfulness, gentleness, and self-control (Galatians 5:22-23). These are the Fruit of the Spirit; positive outcomes of living true to the Spirit of God inside us. But what are they and how can we make ourselves available to them?

Beyond Everyday Virtues

We might think of the fruit of the Spirit as everyday attributes, after all, each fruit describes conditions that society generally encourages us to embody:The love we have for another; the joy of a new baby; the peace of a tranquil setting; our patience in a queue; the kindness we show someone struggling; our generous giving; faithfulness to our religious life or work or marital life; the gentleness we show our children or animal friends, or the self-control we exert under frustrating circumstances. We don't have to look far to see examples of virtues in everyday life. So what makes the fruit of the Spirit different to these positive ways of being?

The various fruit of the Spirit are not simply ethical behaviours or moral goals. They are manifestations of the Holy Spirit's work in us, transforming us into the likeness of Jesus Christ. Unlike virtues we might strive for, these fruit are a grace, a gift from God that deepens our relationship with God. They are the divine energies that assist us to 'become participants of the divine nature.' (2 Peter 1:4)

Divine Energies

'Divine energies?' I hear you ask. 'What are they?' When we speak about 'divine energies', we refer to the way God reveals God's self in the world. Unlike the essence of God, which is beyond our comprehension, divine energies allow us to experience God's presence, power and action in our lives. These energies are uncreated, timeless, and eternal, emanating directly from God. They bring about positive transformation within us as we draw closer to God. This transformation occurs through our participation in and communion with the uncreated energies of the Holy Spirit, the third Person of the Holy Trinity, whose presence offers us sanctification and empowerment to become more and more Christlike.

This divine interaction is not distant or abstract; it is profoundly personal. The divine energies let us be touched by God; our hearts and minds reshaped. This ongoing change in us is a gift of grace, inviting us to participate in God's work and to respond with our own desire for holiness. Through prayer, scripture, the sacraments, and the work of the Holy Spirit, we open ourselves to this sanctifying process.

The Fruit in Scripture

In these daily meditations, you are invited to enter into the richness of scripture, opening yourself to God's Word and deepening your relationship with the Holy Spirit. As you encounter each passage, empty yourself of the day to listen and heed God's Word. You will. Be gently refined by the Spirit —a testament to God's benevolence.

'I am doing a new thing,' (John 14:9) declares the Lord. This transformation is not merely spiritual but encompasses all of you. The Holy Spirit moves our entire being, aligning body and soul towards deification—the process of becoming more like God in love, holiness, and purity through grace and virtuous living. And we begin with the Word of God.

What to Expect

When you embark upon these meditations, you can expect change. Expect spiritual and emotional growth, and a richer, deeper relationship with God inside you. Notice the peace that abounds, along with your increased empathy, compassion and forgiveness. Be aware of how your personal relationships are more blessed, and how the way you connect with people in general has been uplifted. Your speech will be more considered. There will be increased stillness and silence with a desire towards sincerity.

This beauty of authenticity stems from the grace God bestows upon us as we turn more and more towards the uncreated light within us. You will notice this growing sense of truth as you increasingly and unapologetically become more truly you.

Divine Reading

Here's how to approach your meditation. Divine reading, known as *Lectio Divina*, invites you into a deeply contemplative engagement with scripture. This fourfold path will be the jewel of your meditation experience with God.

1. **Read** Approach the daily scripture as you would a dear friend—with an open heart. Read the passage slowly, reverently whispering it aloud multiple times.

2. **Meditate** Now, gently reflect on the passage. This is an almost peripheral state of consciousness rather than a piercing analysis. The passage floats in awareness inviting you to notice how it interacts with aspects of your life. Observe any feelings or emotions that arise here, letting

them rise and fall without following in thought too far.

3. **Pray** Pray the prayer provided or respond to the passage with your own prayer. Then ask God, 'What do you have for me?' Here, you are opening to personal revelation that is unique to you. Pray and listen for a response. Notice any imagery that appears or spontaneous realisations. You will know the Word of God by the interruption in your process, by the newness it brings, the growth it inspires, the 'flavour' of the thought being different to your everyday thinking and the command of it. The holy truth of it. Remember, God never criticises, bullies, or hurts. God will only ever illuminate, reveal, guide and lead you for your good.

4. **Contemplate** With your heart longing to be met, the Spirit of God will respond. Rest now in the presence of

God, allowing any revelation to find home in your heart. In sublime contemplation, the mind slips away, the body ceases to protect, the world quietens as you become a spiritual being. Tears may release the joy of your union with God. Commit to the invitation God gives you. You might give thanks now, ask Jesus for forgiveness, open to healing, praise God or simply rest in the divine presence.

Practice

This is where the fruits are lived and shared. Practical exercises allow God the great adventure of participating in you taking divine illumination into the world. You may like to keep a journal. This is particularly helpful for remembering God's word to you and recording any insights into the application of the Word in your life.

Obstacles

Do not be alarmed if you encounter obstacles to your meditations. And remember that the daily rhythm is a guide only. Go at God's pace, which might not be daily. Here are some examples of potential obstacles:

1. **Mistaking Divine Reading for Bible Study** Being caught up in what words mean or scriptural context keeps you in the head rather than the heart. Let go of study and biblical analysis for the heart to open to divine leading.

2. **Ignoring Life Context** Remember your life context. Be mindful of how the Bible passage relates to certain aspects of your life, and notice the feelings, thoughts and emotions that arise at this time.

3. **Being Cut Off from Emotions** It is important to acknowledge emotions, even the uncomfortable or painful ones. Without dwelling on them, notice how they add to your life context in relation to the scripture passage.

4. **Hurrying** Slow down. Divine reading is not a race but a contemplation. Trust in God's timing. Revelation may not happen in the meditation but days or even weeks later.

5. **Be Kind** How you know and experience God is unique to you. Be kind with yourself in the daily process. Give yourself every measure of harmonious support, even if you fall asleep! Sometimes God simply wants you to rest in the Spirit.

6. **Doubting and Skepticism** Of all the obstacles to God's grace, doubt and skepticism are the most damaging. 'Did I really hear that word?' 'Am I making it up?' 'Was it real?'

Scepticism immediately separates us from God in the moment. Any word God has for us is lost to doubt. Please, allow God, and if you have doubts, take them to a spiritual director or companion, pray on them again or check scripture for a precedent.

7. **Limiting God** It may be tempting to stop the meditations after one revelation. You received a word from God, and amazed by the insight in your life, you rest content in the meditative success. The Holy Spirit continues to do works in and for us. And we must say, 'Yes, here I am God.' The fruit of the Spirit is adventuring to make of your soul a permanent home for divine illumination and for the fruit of the Spirit. Let your prayer be, 'More, Holy Spirit, give me more!'

The Invitation

As you prepare to be blessed this month, set the intention to enter the daily meditation with an open heart, expecting to be shaped and guided by the divine energies that flow from the Spirit of God within you. So, whether you are taking your first steps towards understanding the Spirit's work in your life or continuing to cultivate a deep faith, let your heart be opened now as the raiment of God's transformative authority meets the welfare of your soul in these daily meditations. And may the Lord of all glories bless you and guide you.

Sister Irini

Peace

Your Daily Meditation

Day 1

The Fruit of the Spirit

By contrast, the fruit of the Spirit is love, joy, peace, patience, kindness, generosity, faithfulness.

Galatians 3:15

Prayer

There's a light O' Lord ,wherein you and your promises reside fully and completely. And in that light that rests gently in my heart, there you are. And where you abound, so too lives peace. For You are my Saviour, my Conquer, my world overcomer. You are my Peace. And through that peace, all fruit of the Spirit are brought to bear. Amen.

Joyful Daily Practice

Here are the fruit of the Spirit. Today, as you acknowledge the Holy Spirit's works in you towards living these realities fully in your life, consider what God's peace means to you.

Day 2

The Peace of God

And the peace of God, which surpasses all understanding, will guard your hearts and your minds in Christ Jesus.

Philippians 4:7

Prayer

Lord, when all else comes upon me, and threatens to disrupt the harmony within, I know that the silence you help me to cultivate that sweetens the peace you bring, will hold me steady. Thank you Jesus for this peace that surpasses all understanding. Amen.

Joyful Daily Practice

Sometimes we forget that we can take our requests to God and that in so doing, a great peace comes to us knowing the Lord has our needs in hand. Consider today what you may place before God that you haven't already. Leave it and wait for the Lord's return in this matter.

Day 3

Shout for Joy

Peace I leave with you; my peace I give to you. I do not give to you as the world gives.

John 14:27

Prayer

Today, I pray for that peace Lord, the peace not of the world. I pray to find you in that peace within, to enter into the space you have made just for me wherein I may rest and be emboldened, grow and find comfort, be reassured, and where I am strengthened and know for certain the promises you have made over my life are true and real and present. Amen.

Joyful Daily Practice

What peace do you receive by your faith in Christ that the world does not offer? This is today's invitation: Reflect on the divine presence and purpose in your life.

Day 4

Rejoice in Hope

Therefore, since we are justified by faith, we have peace with God through our Lord Jesus Christ.

Romans 5:1

Prayer

Thank you Lord for the faith you give me by grace. My peace I know is your presence, your person, your love. You are my strength and my foundation. Through your mercy you witness the Father to me, bringing me home to Him. Your peace is the bridge that delivers me into His embrace. Amen.

Joyful Daily Practice

Was there a time when you weren't at peace with God? How has your life changed now? Consider today what peace is afforded your new life in Christ. 'New' because every day you are being remade in Christ's image.

Day 5

Rejoice Always

And let the peace of Christ rule in your hearts, to which indeed you were called in the one body.
And be thankful.

Colossians 3:15

Prayer

Please Lord, help me to love my brethren, those of my church and those of your other churches. Let me feel in my heart of hearts your favour and grace upon all members of your most glorious one body. Let us find commonality amidst diversity, help in need, kindness in difference, and shared love in You Lord. Amen.

Joyful Daily Practice

With so many branches in the Body of Christ that is the Church, where do you find your place? Are you able to look upon other branches of the Body in favour, in loving kinship, as fellow believers and lovers of Christ. Today, reflect on peace amidst diversity in the one body, united in Christ.

Day 6

Unwavering Peace

Those of steadfast mind you keep in peace–in peace because they trust in you.

Isaiah :26:3

Prayer

Oh Holy Spirit, I pray that with so much distraction in my life, you lead me to unwavering faith. Let me know stability and calm as I walk with Jesus. Let me be upheld in His presence that I may know the unshakable quality of His peace in my life. Amen.

Joyful Daily Practice

Peace is both a promise and a gift that comes from faith in God's sovereignty over your life. Enter into this trust in Christ through prayer today. Feel the depth of His peace that fills you. Remember how to recall and enter that peace, and act from that peace towards others.

Day 7

Live Peaceably

If it is possible, so far as it depends on you,
live peaceably with all.

Romans 12:18

Prayer

Jesus, in the world of change where my life is constantly shifting shape, let me live as you lived, welcoming of all in God. Amen.

Joyful Daily Practice

Living peaceably with others often requires great care and compassion, and understanding. Today, think of a relationship that requires more peace and pray into it. It may be someone you know, family or friends or a situation you've become aware of that someone has asked for prayer in helping to resolve. Bring God's peace to the relationship today.

DAY 8

Peace in Believing

May the God of hope fill you with all joy and peace in believing, so that you may abound in hope by the power of the Holy Spirit.

Romans 15:13

Prayer

At times Lord when I do not believe, when my faith is small, not as a mustard seed but as doubt. Make in me a faith filled heart God. Make of me one who believes in your promises that I might partake of your joy and your peace. Amen.

Joyful Daily Practice

This benediction offered by Saint Paul encourages believers to turn to the Holy Spirit to sustain unwavering faith. This is especially true when confronted by challenges. Walk and talk today, anywhere, for any length of time, speaking aloud to the Holy Spirit in peace and praising the Holy Spirit for the peace God delivers to you.

Day 9

Blessed with Peace

May the Lord give strength to his people!
May the Lord bless his people with peace!

Psalm 29:11

Prayer

I know you have many flocks Lord, and that I belong to one only. Let the prayer upon my lips today be for those I do not know, cannot see and may not understand but who are also your people Lord Jesus. Let them be strengthened and know peace, even as I am upheld and peace filled by you. Amen.

Joyful Daily Practice

Today, know that there is strength in peace. Too often we confront people, or we have to be right, have the last word, be stronger than the other person. This psalm is asking you to find strength in peace. Take the path to peace first.

Day 10

Pursue Peace

Pursue peace with everyone,
and the holiness without which no one will see the Lord.

Hebrews 12:14

Prayer

Let my tongue be still in times of argument or quarrel, debate or opposite views. God, let me be still in myself, inviting Jesus into the space within me and around me; space that is filled with you Lord. Amen.

Joyful Daily Practice

Sometimes it is wiser to pursue harmony than it is being right in a conversation. Certainly when the holiness of peace is pursued, silence, no words, may be better than noise and chatter or debate. Sometimes this is necessary to invite the Holy Spirit into the space that such peace invites.

DAY 11

Prince of Peace

For a child has been born for us, a son given to us... and he is named Wonderful Counsellor, Mighty God, Everlasting Father, Prince of Peace.

Isaiah 9:6

Prayer

Father, we thank you for the gift of Your Son, Jesus. In this world, so often filled with turmoil and fear, we look to Jesus as our true light and our unwavering hope. May His wisdom guide us, His strength sustain us, His everlasting love embrace us, and His peace fill our hearts. Amen.

Joyful Daily Practice

Jesus is the Prince of Peace. His authority overcomes sin and death. Today, think on how Jesus gives you spiritual peace that reconciles the broken relationship humanity has with God. It is spiritual peace that leads to eternal peace in the Kingdom of God.

Day 12

Peace At All Times

Now may the Lord of peace himself give you peace at all times in all ways. The Lord be with all of you.

2 Thessalonians 3:16

Prayer

Grant me your peace in all times and ways Lord. May your presence calm my heart and guide me each day. Be with me now. Fill me with your love and world overcoming peace. Amen.

Joyful Daily Practice

When you feel anxious or concerned about a situation, turn to prayer and scripture for God's peace. Who can you offer intercession for by praying peace over them? Pray Jesus' peace into the lives of those in need today.

Days 13

Harvest of Righteousness

And a harvest of righteousness is sown in peace for those who make peace.

James 3:18

Prayer

Lord, let me be a sower of peace, that I might reap a harvest of righteousness. Guide my heart and actions to seek peace with others, to speak gently, and to love deeply. May your peace flow through me, that I may be a light of your goodness in this world. Amen.

Joyful Daily Practice

It is important to know that as one who endeavours to sow peace, there is a harvest you can draw from. And the harvest of peace you find within actively helps a permanent change from reactive behaviours to harmonious and holy behaviours.

Day 14

Counsel Peace

Deceit is in the mind of those who plan evil, but those who counsel peace have joy.

Proverbs 12:20

Prayer

Lord, keep my mind free from deceit and my heart from evil intentions. Help me to be a source of peace and encouragement, so that I may experience the joy that comes from you. Guide my words and actions towards kindness and truth, that I may counsel peace in all things.

Joyful Daily Practice

Have you ever had someone show wisdom and integrity in your life? And then, another who created mischief, lies or deceit. One counsels peace and joy. The other acts against God. Be watchful today as you pray the prayer. Keep yourself without deceit.

Day 15

Mutual Upbuilding

Let us then pursue what makes for peace and for mutual upbuilding.

Romans 14:19

Prayer

Lord, help me to elevate others in your name. Grant me understanding and wisdom, that my words and actions may strengthen those around me. Let me seek out your peace in my life and in others' lives. Amen.

Joyful Daily Practice

What changes would you make to the way you talk, who you talk to, what you say when you speak, when peace becomes your core value. And then, how do you communicate when Christ's peace undergirds all your communication? Contemplate on this today.

Day 16

Kiss Each Other

Steadfast love and faithfulness will meet;
Righteousness and peace will kiss each other.

Psalm 85:10

Prayer

Heavenly Father, I thank you for the meeting place of steadfastness and love in my life. Shape me in your truth that I meet all persons with the kiss of peace. Amen.

Joyful Daily Practice

Reflect on where peace and righteousness 'kiss' in your life. Where do they meet beautifully, and what areas could they be strengthened in. Commit today to promoting both - where the kiss is present, and where work needs doing. Let the prayer of steadfastness and love be on your lips.

Day 17

In Abundance

May mercy, peace, and love be yours in abundance

Jude 1:2

Prayer

Lord Jesus Christ, in your mercy, pour out your peace and love upon me and my loved ones. Let your mercy fill us to overflowing and your love guide our steps. Amen.

Joyful Daily Practice

Take the whole day to receive God's mercy. From the moment you pray until you lay your head upon your pillow, and even then, let the Lord and his love and peace be uppermost in your thoughts; let godly words be upon your tongue; and through his abundant peace, let your actions be holy, and your heart soft and gentle.

Day 18

Peace and Trust

The effect of righteousness will be peace, and the result of righteousness, quietness and trust forever.

Isaiah 32:17

Prayer

O Lord, shape my heart with what is good and right. Let me know trust and faith abounding. Let that trust drive my relations, renew my spirit, grant me newness in all ways. Let it begin with you Lord, and my love for you. Amen.

Joyful Daily Practice

Notice what happens to jealousy, envy, anger, gossiping, judgement, shame, guilt, grief, sadness, fear, despair, lostness, when you feel secure in God; when you know in your heart of hearts that you can trust Jesus, and that all manner of healing, and of peace is available to you in Jesus' name. All those emotions and feelings become quietude.

Day 19

Serve the Lord

I will both lie down and sleep in peace; for you alone, O Lord, make me lie down in safety.

Psalm 4:8

Prayer

This night, Lord, as I turn to sleep, I lie down in your full embrace and know in my heart of hearts that your shield protects me; your steadfast love embraces me. Hallelujah!

Joyful Daily Practice

Regardless of what matters or persons press in against you, your faith in God assures true safety, care and provision. It may not appear as expected but it is the greatest peace and promise of security you will know.

Day 20

To Give Light

To give light to those who sit in darkness and in the shadow of death, to guide our feet into the way of peace.

Luke 1:79

Prayer

Break peace upon me as a river flowing gently over stream Lord. Send me into the day radiant, a light shining before others, witness to life eternal through you, as you guide us in the way of peace ever after. Amen.

Joyful Daily Practice

Jesus is the promise of Zechariah's song of praise here, guiding people out of darkness into the path of peace. As a believer, you too have that grace. Consider the servant heart and the role God may be asking you to aid others out of darkness into peace in Christ's name.

Day 21

He is Our Peace

For he is our peace; in his flesh he has made both groups into one and has broken down the dividing wall, that is, the hostility between us.

Ephesians 2:14

Prayer

In your flesh you bore our separation, our pain and our hostility. Through your sacrifice you tore down the walls between us, and between us and God. Fill my heart this hour that your love may flow into every hardness in me that I may honour your love and by grace be healed. Amen.

Joyful Daily Practice

Think of a trial you have been through or face now. You do not have to face it alone. Jesus Christ offers to stand with you and for you. As He gave His life for you, so too He offers to take your pain and heal you now. He offers to be your strength and to uphold you now. Let Him do so today.

Day 22

Conquering the World

I have said this to you, so that in me you may have peace. In the world you face persecution. But take courage; I have conquered the world!

John 16:33

Prayer

Lord Jesus, you alone are my peace and my victory. Fill me with courage, rooted in the assurance that you have overcome all darkness. Let my heart rest in your strength that I may face each challenge with the boldness of one held by your love. Amen.

Joyful Daily Practice

Through Jesus Christ, you too become a conqueror of the world. This means that whatever trials you face, in Him you will have peace. Offer any fear up to Jesus, who through his crucifixion and resurrection offers you victory over the world; victory over fear.

Day 23

Speaking Peace

Let me hear what God the Lord will speak, for he will speak peace to his people, to his faithful, to those who turn to him in their hearts.

Psalm 85:8

Prayer

O Father, quiet is my voice as my ears turn to you. Quiet are my thoughts as my mind turns to you. Quiet is my heart as my soul reaches for you. Whisper into me your heavenly peace. Amen.

Joyful Daily Practice

Turn to God the Lord today and let God's words comfort and assure you. Let them bring peace.

Day 24

The Mind on the Spirit

To set the mind on the flesh is death, but to set the mind on the Spirit is life and peace.

Romans 8:6

Prayer

Heavenly Father, turn my thoughts from the things of the flesh and of the world that lead to emptiness and sin. Draw me into the life of your divine grace. Let me dwell in the centre of your presence that I may know the purity of peace. Amen.

Joyful Daily Practice

Set your heart to spiritual matters today. Be fed by the Word of God, by God in nature, by a god-filled podcast, sermon, worshipful song. Notice how you light up when turning to the Spirit rather than the physical or worldly. Feel how God in you draws closer in response to your loving attendance.

Day 25

From Joy to Peace

For you shall go out in joy, and be led back in peace; the mountains and the hills before you shall burst into song, and all the trees of the field shall clap their hands.

Isaiah 55:12

Prayer

Lord of all creation, lead me in your joy and peace. Let me look upon your handiwork with wonder and with joy that I may be overflowing with the bounty of your peace. Amen.

Joyful Daily Practice

O glory, glory, so much beauty of God's canvas to behold. Today, take yourself somewhere special; a precious place in nature. Sing, dance, delight for joy and with the peace of heart that nature brings, knowing that the Lord rejoices with you as you bask in God's creation.

Day 26

Loving the Law

Great peace have those who love your law; nothing can make them stumble.

Psalm 119:165

Prayer

Lord Jesus, make of me one who meditates upon your word, for whom your statutes are real and divine, guiding me in my every step. Lift me up in your commandments that I may perceive obstacles before they happen, overcome challenges when they arise, and straighten in your name every step of the way. Amen.

Joyful Daily Practice

A quieter day today, meditating upon God's word. Let the peace that comes from trust and assurance of God in your life, of the promise of God's word on your life, settle into your mind and heart.

Day 27

Unity of the Spirit

Making every effort to maintain the unity of the Spirit in the bond of peace.

Ephesians 4:3

Prayer

Holy Spirit come, help me to partake of your blessing and blessed presence that I may open to your works within me. Let me seek harmony within and without, and breath fresh upon each new encounter in the spirit of peace. Amen.

Joyful Daily Practice

Be aware of how you speak to people today. Avoid divisive words and behaviours in favour of harmony. Being right is not as important as being godly, and being godly is patient, loving, kind, generous. That bond of peace in the Spirit doesn't have to win a disagreement or compete or even accentuate difference of opinion.

Day 28

Live in Peace

Finally, brothers and sisters, farewell. Put things in order, listen to my appeal, agree with one another, live in peace; and the God of love and peace will be with you.

2 Corinthians 13:11

Prayer

Lord Jesus, help me put my life in order according to God's will. Let me have ears to hear and a heart to live peaceably with others. Let me carry your life and your teachings as a beacon to follow and to share. Amen.

Joyful Daily Practice

Ask God to bless your relationships; all of them. Pray this prayer throughout the day. Bring it into your prayer life. The Lord has a way of mending broken relationships, of building new relationships, and of securing current relationships.

Day 29

Sanctifying Peace

May the God of peace himself sanctify you entirely; and may your spirit and soul and body be kept sound and blameless at the coming of our Lord Jesus Christ.

1 Thessalonians 5:23

Prayer

God of peace, make of me a clean spirit. Sanctify me through and through. Let our Lord and Saviour prune all that needs pruning, cut off all that needs severing, and heal all that needs attention. In the time of judgement, may I be found blameless and righteous at the coming of the Lord. Amen.

Joyful Daily Practice

Today, seek God's presence and be honest in your thoughts and behaviours; the kind of honesty that is driven by the Peace of Christ that is unshakable. Consider what Jesus has done for you; the love God has for you. Let this shape you in ways that make pure intentions and all motives.

Day 30

The Lord's Peace

The Lord lift up his countenance upon you, and give you peace.

Numbers 6:26

Prayer

Lord, may your light so shine upon me that I may walk in your love and grace before all persons; and may you walk before me setting the steps for me to follow, a constant companion and shining light on my path to Paradise. Amen.

Joyful Daily Practice

Rest in God's presence. Receive the Peace of Christ through your faith by grace. Ask how you might serve God through this deep, trusting peace. Watch and listen for God's word on this and enter into agreement to do God's will. Take time to reflect on these 30 days and the glory of the Lord who has accompanied you the entire time. Hallelujah!

The Fruit of Peace

This month you have opened your heart to peace. You've allowed God's peace to fill all the places that had need of care. That peace, born of trust in God's goodness, is a gift, a grace—a fruit of the Spirit that gently grounds you in the Lord's love. Yes, it is the bedrock of all other fruit.

And, Holy Spirit gifted peace is not a temporary solace but an abiding grace, an ongoing invitation to dwell in God's care and will. You will notice it now: As you are increasingly rooted in Christ, holy peace reminds you that you are never alone and that God's word over your life is creating and exacting of God's nature. You've come to understand that God's peace isn't just a feeling of calm; it's a dynamic force grounded in

God’s word—His promises and nature—that continually works within you to make you more holy. This divine peace guides you to trust in God's faithful presence and purpose, all the while shaping you into a reflection of God’s own nature.

Through these meditations, each moment of open hearted attention on God; every prayer and pause to dwell in God’s presence towards peace, has been an offering—a surrender that permitted the Holy Spirit to bring peace to your soul, a peace that shields and grows you; a peace that provides sanctifying opportunities. Far from being an abstraction, God’s peace is real, and you will continue to notice it gracing your life in new ways. And you will want to protect it from a world for which peace is increasingly rare. Take time to let that sink in, and to remain true and committed to that peace.

Embracing Peace Beyond this Journey

You might ask, 'Now that these meditations have finished how do I ensure peace stays part of my life?' The good news is that any change that has occurred is permanent. You have partaken of the divine nature and God's quality of peace, and have thereby been transformed!

So, embracing peace going forward is less about what you have to do and more about how to draw on the peace that is now a permanent part of who you are. That means letting peace have expression in your life. One of the best ones to do this is to serve. Serve, serve, serve. And give yourself ongoing opportunities to experience God-given peace.

Continuing in God's Peace

Serve God by serving others. Let your peace speak into the lives of those around you. Whether it is a word from God out of that peace; a quietude that makes room for another; a care that invites someone into God's peace themselves or an active participation in Christ's ministry in the world. Serving others from God's peace will increase your own Holy Spirit fruit.

So too, as you partake of the Holy Sacraments, let peace be a presence you return to over and over. The great stillness that Christ invites you into in the solitude of remembering Him, where it is just you and He in the Holy Communion service, serves divine peace.

Continue to be spiritually fed by a daily prayer life, reading scripture, and taking time with heavenly realities that delight the Spirit for peace.

Then there is nature. We feel at ease in nature as we bathe in the creativity of our Creator. Take walks, breathe deeply, marvel at the handiwork of God, the majesty and beauty. As we rest or bask in nature, we make space for the Holy Spirit to gift us God's peace.

You will have your own blessings that create the atmosphere of rest and quietude, of calm and joy, of wonder and of glee that will make you available to divine peace, and make you able to live out that peace. Promise yourself, promise God, that you will seek out those places and spaces, and ways of being, of serving that foster God's peace.

A Final Blessing of Joy

My prayer is that we all continue to grow in this peace, finding ourselves closer to God's presence and grace.

It is God's comfort and great joy to receive each of us into His peace, to know us in the stillness of our minds, when the seas of torment and struggle are abated, and where we can find Him more readily. My prayer is that it is here, in peace that you will realise your potential to light up and to light another, that your flame may shine brightly in the world, not hidden but fanned anew for generations to come.

God's great joy is to share this with you, to speak with you in the freshness of your peace-filled heart. There, together, you may converse unhindered, unguarded, unafraid. Honesty, openness and truth pervade the space of peace, and out of it all manner of catalyst is created for new discoveries, of self and of other, and of God. What a great privilege for God to know you as you come to know Him; to witness you believing more and more in the great things that you may accomplish together.

Jesus Christ, the Son of God, brought this reality to you. He showed you the way. You are the successive generation to take up His mantle, to claim it your own. What is that? It is the goal of the Father's proximity; the radiance of light into which you and He both step and enjoin one another to become one. It is the glory of you in Him and He in you, and you both together living the fruitful blessing that is this most beautiful life.

Indeed, dear one, the Lord leaves His peace with you—not that it may settle in and be a rested thing, no; that it may be an ever present reminder that the God you love, loves you, is loving you, continues to love you, and the peace you experience is the very fact of that love. Hallelujah!

May God Bless You And Keep You

Your Next Fruit...

Patience, as a Fruit of the Spirit is a steadfast endurance born out of your relationship with Jesus Christ. Not merely the ability to wait, though it is this as well, God-given patience is a holy perseverance that sustains you through trials and hardships. This patience reflects Christ's own long-suffering, offering a calm resilience discarding self for God's will and forbearance. Patience, that is the fruit of the Spirit, empowers you to trust in God's perfect plan, even when the path seems unclear. It grants strength to endure delays and roadblocks, anchoring you in the assurance of God's care and provision. Patience shapes your heart to reflect Christ's gentleness, fostering deep contentment and harmony with others that is at once understanding, accepting and compassionate.

Patience

Your Daily Meditation

Printed in Great Britain
by Amazon

57520601R00056